OPEN EYES

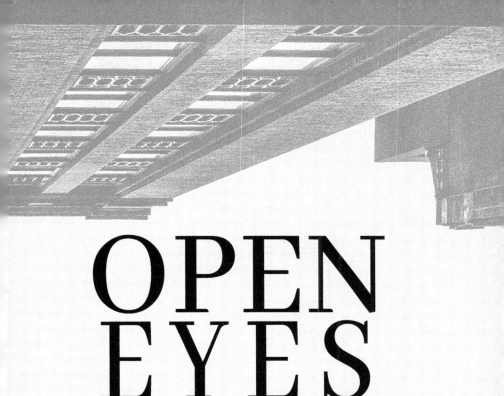

OPEN EYES

JAMILLE EDWARDS

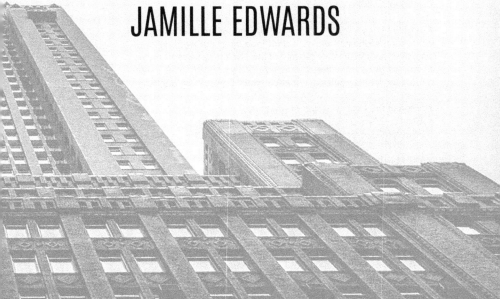

Open Eyes
Copyright © 2024 Jamille Edwards

All rights reserved solely by the author. The author guarantees all contents are original and do not infringe upon the legal rights of any other person or work. No part of this book may be reproduced in any form without the permission of the author. The views expressed in this book are not necessarily those of the publisher.

Printed in the United States of America.
ISBN-13: 979-8-218-51176-0
Library of Congress Control Number: 2024919373

KIH Publishing
Bloomfield, New Jersey

This book is dedicated to my mother, Ameina Edwards, my daughter Tanajah Green, and my aunt Towanda Edwards

CONTENTS

CHAPTER 1 | Open Eyes 1
CHAPTER 2 | The Only Way Out is Through 9
CHAPTER 3 | All That Is Gold
            Does Not Glitter. 17
CHAPTER 4 | Making Dreams Become Reality 25
CHAPTER 5 | Creating Culture Matters 33
CHAPTER 6 | Perseverance. 41
CHAPTER 7 | Time is Everything 49
CHAPTER 8 | The Freedom of Forgiveness 57
CHAPTER 9 | Hustle and Motivation 65
CHAPTER 10 | Manifest the Vision 73
CHAPTER 11 | Keeping It Handsome. 79
CHAPTER 12 | The Marathon Continues 89

ACKNOWLEDGMENTS

Thank You To:
Photographer Malcom Lee
Graphics Design team Shahaad Hinton and Branden
Braxton Custom Suit Tailor & Designer Akief Sheriff

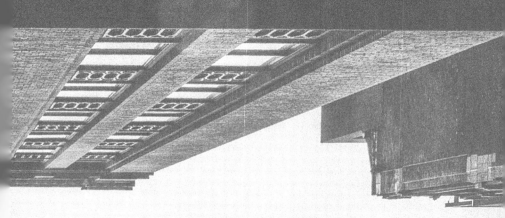

CHAPTER 1
OPEN EYES

"It's not what you look at that matters, it's what you see."

–Henry David Thoreau

THE SECOND A BABY IS BORN, THE DOCTOR HAS TO DO A lot of tests. In the first five minutes, the doctor takes all of the mucus out of its mouth and nose. Then the doctor does a test to make sure the baby can breathe on its own. After that, the umbilical cord is cut so that the baby can be placed in its own warming bed. But the most important thing is that the doctor looks for two things—is the baby crying, and are their eyes open?

When a baby cries, that's not a bad thing; it's actually a good thing. Crying gets the lungs activated. Crying is like an alarm letting everyone in the hospital know, the baby has arrived without a problem. And when a baby opens their eyes, the doctor can put antibiotic in their eyes so that the baby doesn't get an infection. If their eyes never open, they could be blind and nobody knows it. If their eyes never open, they can never adjust to the new world. If their eyes never open, they can't see what they need to see in order to be who they need to be. Think about how hard it is for a baby to adjust to a world like ours. For nine months, the baby has sat in a warm womb, chilling with its mother. The baby hasn't had to talk to anyone, put on clothes, or anything. The baby gets used to its environment, and most babies don't want to leave (I know I wouldn't). But when it's time for them to be born, they have to open their eyes to a brand new world, a whole new normal, and everything changes for them.

I KNOW EXACTLY WHAT IT'S LIKE FOR THE WHOLE WORLD TO CHANGE IN A SPLIT SECOND.

I know exactly what it's like for the whole world to change in a split second. I know what it's like to have your world turn upside down. I also know what it's like to be connected to your mom from the womb, and then one day wake up and realize, she's not there to get you ready for school in the morning. There are so many things that have opened my eyes, and because of that, I have a different perspective about life.

I'LL ALWAYS LOVE MY MOMMA

I was born on March 7, 1991. My mom, Ameina Edwards, raised me and my two siblings the best way she knew how. My sister's name is Mahogany. My brother's name is Orlando. My father wasn't around a lot when I was growing up, but my mother got the help she needed from her eight siblings. She was a jack-of-all-trades. She knew how to turn lemons into lemonade. My mom was a hard worker, and she was so creative. Everything she put her mind to do, she did it and she did it well. Her trade was cosmetology. She loved doing hair, and she loved to help people. From the time that I was a young kid, my mother would take us to the salon with her. The name of the shop was Max's. It was a small shop in Newark, NJ and every day, we would sit in the corner and just watch her work on her clients.

I thought they were just clients but my mother treated everyone that sat in her chair like family. I think that's where I got my creative edge from – watching Mom in the shop. Seeing her work ethic made me want to do the same. **I DIDN'T KNOW, AT THAT TIME, WHAT I WANTED TO DO WITH MY LIFE. BUT I KNEW, WHATEVER I DID, I WAS GOING TO BE THE BEST AT IT.**

whatever I did, I was going to be the best at it.

My mother was my inspiration. She was my motivation. She didn't just teach me to have good manners, she also taught me focus. There are many

> **FOCUS IS THE KEY THAT UNLOCKS EVERY DREAM. IF WE DON'T FOCUS, WE'LL NEVER FINISH.**

people who I talk to every day who want a lot out of life, but they lack focus. They have big dreams and they want to get rich quickly, but focus is the key that unlocks every dream. If we don't focus, we'll never finish. If we don't have a goal in my mind, we'll never reach it. My mother set goals and she made it happen. Every time! Her heart was a heart of gold. She gave the best advice to her clients, and when they needed a listening ear, she would laugh with them, cry with them, and help them anyway she could. The way she treated other people opened my eyes to the way I needed to treat other people. Even if I didn't see eye to eye with them, I learned how to have basic respect for other people. Even if we had a disagreement about something, my mother taught me that there was a right way to do something and a wrong way to do it. It's never cool to talk behind someone's back. It's never OK to bring children into adult problems. It's always right to treat others the way you want to be treated, because you never know when you're going to need someone to help you out.

When my mom's business took off the ground and she started traveling to do hair, my mother didn't let the success get to her head. She was always humble and down-to-earth. She opened my eyes and showed me that the most successful people in the world, are rooted and grounded and relatable. Even to this day, I don't

WHAT DO YOU DO WHEN YOU HAVE ONE ROUTINE, AND THEN, SOMETHING HAPPENS AND MAKES IT ALL CHANGE IN THE BLINK OF AN EYE? get how people can become successful and start acting different. If it was the community that helped you get there, then you shouldn't forget the people that helped you get to the place that you are in, right now. She was grounded and she was welcoming. My mom had an attention-to-detail like none other. I saw her cut hair like she was making art. It was that kind of focus and professionalism that allowed doors to swing wide open for her. For real, she was an artist at heart. Beyond her love for doing hair, she loved music (rap), and even collaborated with Wyclef Jean and Lauryn Hill.

ThIngS BEgAn TO ChAngE

What do you do when your norm changes? What do you do when you have one routine, and then, something happens and makes it all change in the blink of an eye? When I was a kid, I caught the bus to school. And one of the most frustrating things was when the bus route changed, and you didn't know until you got to the bus stop, or you got on the wrong bus. Not only did it waste your time, but it also ruined your day. But the way my life changed, was a lot bigger than a temporary inconvenience. Things started changing fast, and I was too young to really understand it.

As I got older, I started to get a better understanding of how hard my mother was working to make ends meet. My mother raised all three of her kids without any assistance from anybody. My siblings and I shared one bedroom; my brother and I had a bunk bed on one side of the room and my sister's bed was on the other. If we were poor, I didn't know it. If we were a part of a "statistic," I didn't feel it. All I felt was love. I loved being home with her.

AND JUST LIKE THAT, MY MOTHER WAS GONE. IT ALL HAPPENED SO FAST.

My mother always reminded us that our hard work at school and at home would be rewarded. She would even promise us gifts at Christmas from Santa to make us do right. My siblings and I would do our best, all year round, because we knew that Christmas was coming. And days before Christmas, we would stay up late to see and hear our mom creeping around the house with our aunties wrapping and hiding our gifts. She was an angel from above. She didn't need to brag about her drive. We saw it for ourselves. She was determined to make sure we had all we needed.

When I turned 5 or 6, I started to realize my mother's health started to decline. Even though we were kids we could tell something was not right. She wasn't walking as fast. She would call us in to help her do small things. She would call out of work from time to time, and that wasn't like her at all. A little while later, my mother was diagnosed with stomach cancer and the three of us were sent to live with Mahogany's grandparents. I didn't really understand what cancer was at the time; I was too young. But I did know that something wasn't right. A short time after we found out she had cancer, my mother started chemotherapy but her body did not respond well to it. Instead of getting better, things got worse. And when it was clear that she was not getting any better, my siblings and I would go to the hospital after school to spend time with her.

The last time we went to the hospital, the doctors called a code blue, and rushed to her bedside. They revived her three times, but the last time, she didn't come back to us. And just like that, my mother was gone. It all happened so fast. Life, as I knew it, would never be the same. How does a kid process the loss of his mother? Who is going to feed him in the morning, and tuck him in at night? Who is going to tell him to get up and take a shower, and then double check to make sure that he did it? The hospital scene was a mess. My uncle started fighting the doctors, and got locked up. My family was in pieces. Before I knew it, I was separated from my sister Mahogany. She was sent back to live in PA with her grandparents, and I barely saw her. Orlando was sent to live with his dad, and I started living with my Aunt Kianna. In a moment, our entire norm changed. We went from going to school together, eating dinner together, to not speaking for weeks at a time.

I think I cried, but I don't really know. All I know is that my mother's death opened my eyes. It opened my eyes to how much I needed her. It opened my eyes to how much I needed love. My mother's life and death taught me how important it is to make every day count. If people know me now, they will tell you that I don't believe in days off. I don't believe in sleeping in. I got my grind from mother. I got my determination from my mother. If my mother could still take care of us even while she was sick, there is nothing that can stop me from taking care of my family.

But all of these made me a different person. The most important years of a child's life is the time between

OPEN EYES

elementary school and high school. My mom wasn't there for any of that. My mom didn't meet my first girlfriend. She didn't watch me graduate from high school. She wasn't here to kiss my daughter when she was born. And she didn't get a chance to read my first book. But this book, Ma, is for you. Without you, I wouldn't be half the man I am, and I hope my life will prove to you how grateful I am that you gave me life, and opened my eyes.

CHAPTER 2
THE ONLY WAY OUT IS THROUGH

"You must be willing to accept the fact that pain is a part of the process of revelation."

—Stanley Crouch

WHEN I STARTED GOING TO HIGH SCHOOL, I STARTED TO get into the gym heavy. At first, I wanted to work out so that I could get a scholarship. I was really athletic in school so I did a little bit of everything—football, basketball, wrestling—you name it, I did it. I loved to be active. I got my competitive edge from my mom, and I loved to be a part of a team that was winning. But the only way to win on the field, was to work out in the gym. So I went to the gym to get stronger, and to build stamina.

I ain't gonna lie—at first, it was hard. But then, I developed a hunger for it. I developed an appetite for the pain that came along with the gym. The pain didn't feel good but I knew it was *for* good. And every time I felt pain, I knew that my muscles were growing. My mindset started to change. I didn't go to the gym for the easy reps. I went looking for the challenge. And If I went to the gym, and I didn't feel sore, I knew I hadn't pushed myself hard enough. I knew I had more reps in me, and I knew that I was playing it safe.

ARE YOU PLAYInG IT SAFE?

You'd be surprised how many people are playing it safe in life. They are wired to own businesses, but they play it safe and just go to college, get a safe job, and live in a safe neighborhood. Now, look, I'm not knocking college. I went to college myself. But I also know that college is not for everybody. Some people will find their success down that road, and some people won't. But whichever road you decide to go down, you can't avoid the pain. There will be pain in school because you have to stay

THERE IS NO PROMISE WITHOUT PAIN. THERE IS NO PRIZE WITHOUT PAIN. up all night and study for tests. There will be pain in business because a lot of times, you won't know what you're doing at first. There will be pain in the military because you have to go to boot camp and be willing to put your life on the line for your country if they send you out to battle. There will be pain in parenting because you will raise a child that may one day become ungrateful and unthankful. There is no promise without pain. There is no prize without pain. And what I learned, after my mom passed, was this: the only way out of the pain is to go THROUGH the pain.

YOU CAn GET THROUGH THIS

The same way I had to breathe harder, yell louder, and pull from my soul when I was in the gym, I had to do the same thing in life. As I said earlier, why my mom died, I moved to Orange, NJ to stay with my grandmother. But every day I had to hop on the bus to get to school in Newark at West Side High School Newark Public Schools were not the same as other districts. High school is hard enough as it is. When kids go to high school, they are going through a lot of changes. Their body is changing. Their needs are changing. They have to deal with the pressure of getting ready for college, or figuring out what they will do when they get out into the real world. They are no longer a kid, and they can't "get by" off of the excuses they used in elementary school. They are in the hallway of life's decisions. The rest of their life will depend on how they handle high school.

OPEN EYES

Some people go on to get scholarships because of what they did in high school. Some people drop out and never get a good paying job because of high school. The pressure is serious, but what happens when you end up going to a high school without your mom? What happens when you go to a school where people are fighting, selling drugs, and involved in gangs? I'll tell you what happens—you learn at a young age, to get through the pain on a daily basis.

Everybody who came to school with me, carried some pain. In high school, everybody was affiliated with a gang. And those of us who weren't in a gang, got picked on constantly. The gangs were the "it" thing when I was younger, and every day, someone was getting beat up, or had to fight to protect themselves.

Imagine going to school, leaving the pain of your household—either your dad not in the house, or your loved one is gone—and then you get to school and have to deal with initiation, bullying, and all types of dumb shit. It was no joke out there. And some months, it got so bad that we had to leave practice early and get back home before dark because of safety concerns. I even had a few coaches take me home to make sure I was OK since I lived so far from the school. It was pain on top of pain, and it's true what they say—*hurt people hurt people.* When someone has been hurt by another person, all they know to do sometimes is hurt people.

> SOME PEOPLE GO ON TO GET SCHOLARSHIPS BECAUSE OF WHAT THEY DID IN HIGH SCHOOL. SOME PEOPLE DROP OUT AND NEVER GET A GOOD PAYING JOB BECAUSE OF HIGH SCHOOL.

High school opened my eyes to see the truth about school. A lot of kids were carrying more than their books to class every day. They did the best they could, but they couldn't ace the test because they had to worry about how they were going to eat the next day. Some of the freshman in my high school were working part-time jobs just to make sure the bills got paid in their house. How are you going to succeed when you have to work a 5-hour shift after school, and then you only sleep for 3-4 hours before you have to get up and go back to school? I had to work longer hours than that.

Some people rose to the occasion and did better with their lives. They became doctors, lawyers, athletes, politicians, and some of them came back to Newark to help the city. But a lot of people didn't make it. I lost a lot of friends in high school because of gang violence and senseless fights. My boy, Henry, got setup by his girlfriend, and the next thing we heard, he had been robbed and killed. Henry was only 16 years old. My other boy, stole a car and crashed into a pole driving 90mph. His family was Hispanic, and some days we would walk in school and when we saw a crowd of people crying by the principal's office, we knew somebody had died. This was real pain. But the only way out of the pain was THROUGH.

> HIGH SCHOOL OPENED MY EYES TO SEE THE TRUTH ABOUT SCHOOL. A LOT OF KIDS WERE CARRYING MORE THAN THEIR BOOKS TO CLASS EVERY DAY.

KEEP GOInG

I couldn't stop. I couldn't give up. I had goals. I had a vision for my life, and I needed to work hard on the football team so that I could get a scholarship into a Division 1 school. That was my goal. I knew I wanted to do something major, but I didn't really know what that was yet.

> **IN THE MIDST OF A LOT OF PAIN, THERE WERE POSITIVE PEOPLE THAT HELPED ME TO CHANGE MY PERSPECTIVE.**

All I knew was that I was good at sports, so I focused on that. But the harder I worked on the football team, the more pain I experienced because by the end of my high school career, I had lost 4-5 good brothers that played on the team with me.

Nobody taught me about grieving. Hell, I didn't even really cry when my mother passed. But if I reached out to talk to someone in school, I couldn't really tell the truth because even the best kids on the team were in gangs. Man, it was crazy. One day, they would be playing and the next day they would be locked up. Their parents didn't go to bail them out—you know who got them out? The coaches! Thank God most of our coaches were cops, SWAT officers, or detectives; so they did their best to keep us on the straight and narrow, but it was hard to get these kids off the streets.

Beyond the gangs, there was even more pain to deal with when you went home to a drug addicted mother, or an alcoholic father. But all was not lost. High school taught me to open my eyes and see the light at the end of the tunnel. In the midst of a lot of pain, there were positive people that helped me to change my perspective.

My high school brother and mentor, Pierre Oscar, really opened my eyes. He was my athletic guidance counselor and a lifetime member of Alpha Phi Alpha. Pierre Oscar led by example. He taught me how to persevere. He taught me how to conduct myself professionally. He brought programs to the school that helped us to rise above our community. One program was called "Go to high school, Go to college." He didn't allow us to settle. The goal of this program was to help men transition into college education. He had another program called "Voteless people to hopeless people" which was a program that taught us the importance of learning and voting. I didn't realize how crucial voting was as a black man until my mentor opened my eyes.

Another program he introduced to us was a program called "Project Alpha" which was an initiative focused on supporting the elderly. None of us were thinking about any of that until he opened our eyes. He helped us to see that the world was bigger than sports. He helped us to see that we could really be a part of the change we wanted to see, and for that, I will forever be grateful.

WHEN PEOPLE COME INTO YOUR LIFE TO LEVEL UP YOUR LIFE, BE GRATEFUL. PAY IT FORWARD. SOMETIMES ALL YOU NEED IS ONE PERSON TO HELP YOU GET THROUGH THE PAIN.

When people come into your life to LEVEL UP your life, be grateful. Pay it forward. Find someone that you can level up, and do it so that someone else can be better. Don't do it so that people can applaud you. Do it because you owe it to your community to raise the bar, and be the change. I didn't have a close relationship with my dad, but I did have my mentor. And my mentor had me. Sometimes all you need is one person to help you get through the pain. When you find that person, appreciate them for life. They are going to help you to get through the best of times and the worst of times.

CHAPTER 3

ALL THAT IS GOLD DOES NOT GLITTER

"Fail early, fail often, but always fail forward. The difference between average people and achieving people is their percep- tion of and response to failure."

-John Maxwell

I HAVE HAD A LOT OF OBSTACLES IN MY LIFE. WHEN I LOOK back over everything, sometimes it's amazing that I'm still standing. I know everybody has obstacles, but sometimes it seems like obstacles and challenges used to stalk me. Most people probably feel like that though. Because every person experiences let-downs, breakdowns, breakups and upsets. It's part of life. Obstacles don't make any of us special or different. The ones who stand out are people who learn how to deal with it and keep stacking along the way. As a matter of fact, most of us learned what's most important in life during the dark days, not in great situations. We only grow for real when we're up against the wall.

WE ONLY GROW FOR REAL WHEN WE'RE UP AGAINST THE WALL.

It's human nature to kind of coast when things are going well. I remember as a kid, I wasn't thinking about school when my grades were okay. As long as everything was decent and my mom wasn't getting on me, I chilled. It was only when a "D" or "F" hit that I started putting some time in. Trying to make sure everything was cool before report card time. That's how we are as people. When your lady is happy, bills are paid, friends and family are cool, it's easy to just chill. We go on autopilot kind of. Sometimes when things are great, we stop grinding and we stop trying. But when the heat turns up that's often the time when we show the world what we are truly made of. As a matter of fact, if you want to know what a man is really made of, check him out the day after the bottom falls out from underneath him.

FIRED InTO MY FUTURE

When I really think about it, it's amazing that I'm a barber. To tell the truth, that was the last thing on my radar at one point in time. A lot of people don't know this, but I had my heart set on law enforcement when I was growing up. I got the job and everything.

Back in 2016, I got hired as an armed officer in the courthouse and it was everything. I still remember the first day: I was hype. Went in on top of the world. Had landed my dream job. Was making good money and I just knew that in no time, I would be running things. You couldn't tell me nothin'!

It was cool while it lasted. But it didn't last. I was only on the force for two years when things turned. I was good at my job too, that's what made it so hard. I was great at the job, was planning on moving up, everything was lovely. But you can't control circumstances all the time. Not too long after I was hired, I started hearing whispers about budget issues. I ignored it and just did my job and minded my business. Eventually it turned out to be true though. The economy hit, and as quick as I had gotten the job, one day out of the blue they announced budget cuts. We all know how it goes: Last hired, first fired. Most rookies got laid off because of the cuts and I was one of the ones who got the boot. Just like, that my dream job went right down the drain.

DREAM AS IF YOU'LL LIVE FOREVER
LIVE AS IF YOU'LL DIE TODAY.

What do you do when a dream dies? How do you keep going when the woman you think you want to marry, ends up with someone else? Or when the position you think is for you, goes to someone less qualified than you? It's not an easy thing to get up and keep pressing, but I learned a long time ago that all that is gold doesn't glitter.

> IT'S NOT AN EASY THING TO GET UP AND KEEP PRESSING, BUT I LEARNED A LONG TIME AGO THAT ALL THAT IS GOLD DOESN'T GLITTER.

Sometimes, we want what we want until we open our eyes. And granted, anyone who has ever lost a job knows how much it hurts. Like always, it was a major hit to my ego and it definitely hit my pockets. The checks stopped coming but the bills didn't. When I lost my job, my car got repossessed and my accounts were in the negative all of the time due to no income. But on top of those normal things that come with losing any job, there was some deeper hurt with this one. This wasn't just a job for me, this was the thing I really wanted to do in the world at that time. I thought this job was the only job for me. It took a while to come back from feeling almost hopeless. It was even harder to shake the sense of failure. So many people knew how much I had wanted that job. People

> WHEN MY DREAM DIED, I HAD TO WAKE UP AND GET TO WORK. I COULDN'T SIT AROUND AND DO NOTHING. I HAD TO PUT SOMETHING TOGETHER FAST.

saw how happy I was when I started, and now I had to deal with those same people seeing me lose it.

When my dream died, I had to wake up and get to work. I couldn't sit around and do nothing. I had to put something together fast. I didn't know exactly what to do, but I sat and thought about what I *could* do. Whenever life boxes you out like that, always take a minute and think. Think about the options you have because you always have something! Think about the talents and experiences you have. Any good Spades player will tell you, if you pay attention to what's in your hand long enough you can find something to play. For me, I decided to go back to something I had always been good at but never really thought much about. Hair. I had cut hair before and was pretty good, but I always saw it as a side hustle. I figured working in the courthouse would be my bread and butter. But getting laid off forced me to go back to what my gift really was. So I started cutting again.

SLOW DOESn'T MEAn nO

I definitely have to say this for anybody who might think you can somehow skip steps in the process of finding your "golden spot." I'm using the term golden spot to refer to that sweet spot, that perfect place that's made just for you. It's like it's got a hot yellow spotlight shining on it, just for you. I figured out over time that barbering is mine. But I didn't figure it out overnight. As a matter of fact, when I started cutting again

> EVERYTHING STARTED OFF SLOW, BUT I DIDN'T STOP. INSTEAD OF GETTING FRUSTRATED AND BOWING OUT, I DECIDED TO PUT IN THE WORK.

> **IF YOU WANT TO HAVE ANY REAL SUCCESS IN LIFE YOU HAVE TO LEARN HOW TO GO SLOW AND NOT LET IT STOP YOU.**

after getting laid off, the first few months weren't pretty at all. I didn't go right into full-time with a full clientele and a great spot in a shop. I didn't make top dollar. As a matter of fact, I went from making pretty good money full-time position I had to just getting a few heads here and there when I first started cutting for real. I was part-time and it was a struggle. Everything started off slow, but I didn't stop. Instead of getting frustrated and bowing out, I decided to put in the work. I worked on my cutting technique. I built my clientele. I didn't stop at the yellow light, I just respected the moment I was in and I slowed down. Not forever, just until I got a green!

This is something we all have to learn and quick. If you want to have any real success in life you have to learn how to go slow and not let it stop you. Remember what I said in the last chapter, "keep going." People in business who study and teach people about entrepreneurship, talk all the time about how important it is to keep going. Most businesses fail very early. Sometimes it's just because the businessman or businesswoman doesn't know how to keep going. You can't get anything out of this life if you give up every time you fall down or take a loss. When your back is up against the wall, the best thing you can do is roll up your sleeves and start pushing. If movement starts slow, don't get discouraged or distracted.

> **A LOT OF PEOPLE ARE AFRAID OF FALLING DOWN, BUT ON THE GROUND IS SOMETIMES WHERE YOU FIND YOUR PURPOSE.**

Take the slow route; it still gets you to the finish line. Even if it looks like you failed, learn the lesson and keep moving forward.

FAIL FORWARD

A lot of people are afraid of falling down, but on the ground is sometimes where you find your purpose. Being laid off was one of the hardest chapters of my life to relive, but it got me in place for my real call. What we see as failures or closed doors can sometimes be the best way to find an even better path. Losing a job, failing a class, getting a divorce, getting dropped from a contract; none of these things are the end of the world. Open your eyes and see the failure as a lesson. It isn't final. But it has come to teach you something. If you can learn to fall and get back up, you are ahead of the game. See, every person you ever meet will have moments when they are down for the count. It's part of the game. But the people who will succeed in the end are the ones who aren't too ashamed to get up, dust off and keep on swinging. We are all going to fail at some point in life, but if you do, at least fail forward.

CHAPTER 4
MAKING DREAMS BECOME REALITY

"The biggest adventure you can ever take is to live the life of your dreams."

-Oprah

THE OLD SAYING GOES, "NOTHING COMES TO A SLEEPER but a dream." It's kind of true. Just dreaming alone doesn't get you much in this world. That doesn't mean that dreams aren't important though. The truth is that mostly everything that's worth something started out as a dream in somebody's head. There's nothing wrong with having dreams, goals and visions. But there is something wrong with stopping there. Dreaming a dream is nothing if you don't wake up and start making it a reality in the morning.

When my eyes opened and I saw that all I really had was my dream and my grind, I started making changes. All of my friends in high school were focused on partying and girls; I was focused on setting goals. I knew I had something to bring to the world and I wasn't going to let anything stop me. Thanks to my moms, I had a work ethic like none other. I caught two to three buses to work at ShopRite. I worked the late shift and then ran home to sleep for a few hours before I had to hop the bus, go to school and then stay after for football practice. I was determined to make every dream a reality, but that didn't happen for me because I dreamed it. It happened for me because of my determination.

Anybody who isn't determined will not succeed. Point blank period. Anybody who does more talking about their goals without a plan to make it happen, is only trying to impress people. Dreams

> **THERE'S NOTHING WRONG WITH HAVING DREAMS, GOALS AND VISIONS. BUT THERE IS SOMETHING WRONG WITH STOPPING THERE.**

are important but determination is key. Listen, everybody loves Dr. King today, and we are all grateful for his work. Everybody remembers and loves the "I Have a Dream" speech. But having the dream wasn't the end of his work. Dr. King spent years of his life doing the work to make his dream become a reality. And it wasn't just him. Coretta Scott King, E.D. Nixon, Rosa Parks, all worked with him in Montgomery to bring his dream to life. And across the country and the world there were more people working the dream. The dreamer and the dream are important, but the work is crucial. What is the work that you're doing to make this thing come alive? I know you want to be in the NBA but how often do you work out? There are a million great young athletes out there. What makes you stand out? I have so many clients that want to get into the music industry, but they aren't working their local market. You can get impressed and distracted by the social media glam all day, but the world won't respect you if the neighborhood doesn't. The glam is good, but at the end of the day, priorities are more important than parties. I always knew this as a kid, but one day, I had to get up and actually work my dream.

> **YOU CAN GET IMPRESSED AND DISTRACTED BY THE SOCIAL MEDIA GLAM ALL DAY, BUT THE WORLD WON'T RESPECT YOU IF THE NEIGHBORHOOD DOESN'T.**

WORKInG THE DREAM

I remember when I first decided that I was going to stick with cutting hair long-term. After the layoff, and starting

> **IT DOESN'T JUST COME TO YOU, YOU HAVE TO HUNT SUCCESS DOWN.**

back to cutting again, things definitely didn't start off great. First off, I didn't go from lay-off to full-time automatically. I started part- time, and I mean *really* part-time. Like part of the time it felt like no time, part-time. I had been giving everything to my full-time job, and spent a lot of time and energy preparing before that. So I didn't have a huge clientele built up. Also, I didn't have a great space to work in. I didn't have all of the things I needed to cut well. So I had to work my way into where I wanted to be. That meant that, for a season, I had to grind like my life depended on it. Now, we all talk about grinding all the time, but this was a different level. I'm not just talking about working hard – I still work hard and always have. But there was a time when I had to seriously work the dream like everything was going to go down the drain if I didn't. Challenges like being part-time and needing to get known made me go hunt for success. It doesn't just come to you, you have to hunt success down. And challenges helped to pave the path for me. Having to constantly sit down and think about a new way. Having to always think through problems and come up with a creative solution. It all got me used to thinking and working smarter.

That's the gift of problems. Sometimes we think of problems as all bad, but really they help teach us a lot. Being part-time when I first started out allowed me to grow as my clientele grew. While I was working on my craft I was

> **WHEN YOU HAVE A DREAM, YOU HAVE TO BE WILLING TO DO WHATEVER IT TAKES TO BRING IT TO LIFE.**

able to invest time in the stuff that nobody sees. Being great at anything requires two things: time and practice. And those hungry days early on, gave me plenty of time to become the best I could be. During my part- time days I didn't see it as an opportunity to chill and relax. I didn't see down time as a vacation. When I wasn't cutting I was watching master-barbers, or drumming up business. When I wasn't doing those things, I was going to barbering shows and checking out new techniques on the internet. I worked more when I was part-time than most people work two jobs. I knew my dream wasn't just going to come to me. I had to wake up and work.

HIT 'EM UP UnTIL YOU COME UP

Everybody knows somebody who is always hitting folks up for something. It's the stereotype we have for small business owners especially. But as much as people might make fun of it, it's part of the territory. When you have a dream, you have to be willing to do whatever it takes to bring it to life. When that dream is a business and involves other people, you can't be too proud to ask. People won't just automatically know about your service or business or product. You have to get the word out and you have to convince people of the value. So that means you can't skip steps. You have to major, at least in the first few years, in marketing, branding and building capacity. Let's break those down, starting with marketing.

The American Marketing Association says that marketing is "the activity, set of institutions, and processes for creating, communicating, delivering, and exchanging offerings that have value for customers, clients, partners, and society at large." Investopedia, a resource for people

> **IT'S NOT ENOUGH TO BE IN THE RIGHT CIRCLES IF YOU'RE NOT DOING THE WORK.**

who want to create and invest in businesses, says that marketing is about "activities undertaken by a company to promote the buying or selling of a product or service. Marketing includes advertising, selling and delivering products to consumers or other businesses." So when I say that you have to major in marketing from jump, I mean you have to get the word out by every means. You should believe in yourself and your product or service so much that you don't mind hitting up everybody you come into contact with. If you know that you have something to offer, offer it. Marketing means getting the word out to as many people as possible, as often as possible, the best way possible. So nothing should be off limits when marketing. If you're on social media, it shouldn't take long at all for anybody in your feed to know about your work. Word of mouth, advertising, use it all.

But don't forget this part. One of the biggest parts of marketing that people don't think about is doing a great job every time. A great product, professionalism, and consistent delivery leads to the best kind of marketing: word-of-mouth. When I was starting out, I started attending network events to get to know more people in the industry. What made this work for me was that I also was doing world-class work and doing it consistently. As I met people they were helping me to get the word out about what I was doing. Catch that. It's not enough to be in the right circles if you're not doing the work. But the more I met people, the more they could help me access new investors and clients. And they could vouch for me because they knew my work.

My clientele blew up in little to no time because all of my clients were my best marketers. I invested time and money into traditional marketing, but I got the most out of word-of-mouth. Nothing is more effective marketing than a happy customer. More and more people started telling their friends how tight my fades were and how sharp my lines were. That meant more customers and more opportunities.

> **KNOW WHO YOU ARE AND WHAT YOU WANT TO DO. FOCUS WHAT YOU DO AND HOW YOU MARKET IT SO THAT PEOPLE CAN EASILY RECOGNIZE YOU.**

GETTInG BRAnD nEW

Branding is important too. Businessdictionary.com defines branding as "The process involved in creating a unique name and image for a product in the consumers' mind, mainly through advertising campaigns with a consistent theme. Branding aims to establish a significant and differentiated presence in the market that attracts and retains loyal customers." This means that branding is about you being you. Know who you are and what you want to do. Focus what you do and how you market it so that people can easily recognize you. Think about it: when you see a golden arch and a red background, you know it's McDonald's. When you see that apple with a bite out of it, you know it's an Apple product. That's good branding.

But branding is also about sticking to what you want to do. Make sure everything you do is recognizable. Being branded means you don't do 10 different things. Cooking burgers, cutting hair, power washing houses and doing taxes might seem like it would make a lot of money, but it's too much. Stick with your gift, build your brand.

After that, build capacity. Build slowly and smart. Anybody in any business knows that you don't spend all of the profits. You put money back into the business. That's what building capacity is. It's gonna look different for different businesses. If you're a barber who rents a chair, you are mostly gonna build by buying great tools and marketing for more and better clients. If you own a shop, you need to be constantly making the shop better. In the 21st Century nobody wants to go to a dirty, dusty, non-decorated shop. Put some character into the shop. Maintain things well. Offer services that match the kind of shop you want to be. Don't think you can be a top of the line shop unless you start offering top of the line amenities. Build on the dream, brick by brick.

CHAPTER 5
CREATING CULTURE MATTERS

"The black skin is not a badge of shame, but rather a glorious symbol of national greatness."

– Marcus Garvey

WHAT DO YOU THINK ABOUT WHEN you hear the word culture? Some people think culture means stuff that is proper and formal, like plays and the orchestra. Some

> **CULTURE IS ABOUT THE CHARACTER OF SOMETHING.**

people think about race and religion and things like that. Culture can mean a few different things, but it always has to do with what something is like. Culture is about the character of something. When you hear the word Jamaican you might think about jerk seasoning, reggae, ginger beer and Marley. That's culture. But it's not just countries and races that have cultures. Every business has one too. The kind of music you play in your shop. The kind of cuts you do. The colors of the paint and the decorations. Everything is part of your culture. But culture definitely goes deeper than wall art and clippers. It's what people feel when they walk in the door. Some of it is what you can see and touch. But some of it is just that sauce that you can't really describe.

Think about Black people. Our culture can't be described easily. It's more than the food we eat and the music we love. When you hear Black people sing or talk, there's something there underneath the surface. Culture is about what has accumulated over time. Culture is more than just singing the words of the song; it's how you sing it. It's why certain people can sing a song or read a poem and you feel nothing. But when we get a hold of it, it sounds like something completely different. That's culture, that thing you can't really define or describe, but you can't miss it when you see it.

GET YOUR CULTURE On

Building KIH's (Keeping It Handsome) culture didn't happen overnight. Culture is built brick by brick. And you

YOU GET WHAT YOU CREATE.

can't let up when you're building it. It was a long road from cutting a head here and there (at William Paterson University) to building my own brand. Some of the process was really about doing things the right way over and over. That's what building culture is. Marketing and branding work together to make something that people expect. What they expect and experience when they sit in your chair, that's culture.

Different businesses create different cultures. And culture is serious when it's created. Once you have a culture going, it's hard to change it. For instance, if you hire all young workers and blast hip-hop all day, your culture is going to be young and innovative. That might be what you want. It might not. But what and who you bring in is going to eventually turn your shop or business or service into something specific. And if you have that young culture, it's gonna be hard to get clients in their 60s. If you play smooth jazz, stay on barbers and customers about not cussing and keep your shop bright and well-stocked, culture will be older and chill. You get what you create.

Early on, I knew I wanted my culture to emphasize excellence and professionalism. From the early days

CULTURE FOLLOWS THE CULTURE- MAKER.

cutting part-time while in college I worked at that. Every day after class I went to my second school. I spent hours every day on Youtube and across the Internet finding new techniques and the best clippers. I took my craft seriously and worked at it. This shaped culture all along my journey. So that when I went full time and when I got my own space, every step of the way the culture reflected who I was. Culture follows the culture-maker. Even now, part of my culture is a "the sky is the limit" mentality. Also, creativity is part of the culture. I'm a social media person because of my age. I used that. I built my culture through social media in some ways. Instagram and Facebook are all about crisp angles, good photos, and modern looks. So I have focused on those things and that has made my social game strong. Part of being successful in this generation requires being open to researching and communicating on social media.

KEEPInG IT HAnDSOME

My major brand, Keeping it Handsome, LLC is all about confidence and elegance. That's the culture I have created around me. As an entrepreneur and educator, I am always encouraging men to find a barber who makes them feel confident. Men need a partner in their barber. Somebody who can see your vision for yourself and create it. So everything I do is around that. We give our clients first class service, but at the same time, we encourage them to represent themselves freely. We don't force people to like what we like, we help support their vision and their version of excellence. My goal is to provide services that

> **YOU CAN'T TEACH WHAT YOU DON'T KNOW. AND YOU DON'T KNOW IT IF YOU HAVEN'T DONE IT YOURSELF.**

> **SO LONG BEFORE YOU BECOME PROFITABLE, IT'S IMPORTANT TO HAVE PEOPLE.**

make men into better men by improving how someone feels about themselves. Whenever we feel better inside, it shows up on the outside. We also believe that our craft is distinguished from others because it is deeply rooted in who we are as a people. This is why I endeavor to help barbers to become real artists who can do what their customers want. Helping barbers to make their space creative and open. Doing interviews that help people gain keys for leveling up. Building KIH is a lot about knowing my own brand and culture and sharing it with the world. You can't teach what you don't know. And you don't know it if you haven't done it yourself.

My purpose is much bigger than making money and growing my brand. My purpose is to create culture and unity within the individuals I meet. I remember when I was cutting in collegeat William Paterson. I remember how hard it was for my boys to find a great barber. Every man knows that feeling. When you move to a new place or your barber moves or something else happens. You show up to barbershop after barbershop, trying to find the right artist. You know what you want your hair to look like. You know how it feels to have a great barber and to get up out of the chair feeling good. But it's hard to find it again. Every time you sit down in a new chair, you're risking your hairline! So I started out because I wanted to help people find that feeling we all love. And now, part of my work is to do it but also to teach it. KIH is about doing what I do outside of my own city. It's about helping people all over to do the same thing and feel the same feeling. So everywhere I go, I'm working to build barbers.

BEFORE THE DRIP, BEFORE THE MONEY, PEOPLE HAVE TO BUY INTO YOU WHEN YOU CAN'T OFFER MUCH YET.

YOUR nETWORK IS YOUR nET WORTH

Since culture is about what you can't create quickly or alone, people are important. Since marketing is strongest when it is done by word-of-mouth, people are important. Since a great business will fall if you don't have enough people to help you meet the demand, people are important. So long before you become profitable, it's important to have people. Faithful employees, satisfied customers, peers and mentors who help you grow. Your network is your net worth when you're building. Part of the reason is because you need people to buy into your vision long before you can bring it to pass all the way. Most people who get a great idea can't get it off the ground alone. That was me. I had a gift and the passion, but that isn't enough in today's world. There are too many competitors to think anything is gonna blow up without effort and a team. When I was cutting hair in dorms, I needed brothers to trust me with their hair. When I first picked the clippers back up after getting laid off, I needed people to take a chance spending their money with an amateur. Eventually I needed people to leave their

> BE LOYAL TO YOUR CLIENTS AND YOUR CLIENTS WILL BE LOYAL TO YOU.

barbers to support me. And it's hard for a Black man to leave his barber. The only way it worked was because I had some people who believed in me. Long before I had 15,000 followers and a national brand, people saw me. They saw something in me. They bought into the vision before they could see it. A saying I live by: "People don't buy what you do, they buy why you do it." That's definitely true when you start off. People who see your drive and hustle will save you when you could fall apart. People who give a huge tip because they know you're just starting out. People who give your name to a big name client. Before the drip, before the money, people have to buy into you when you can't offer much yet.

This is why loyalty is life. If you want to build or do anything, create a culture of loyalty. Take note of the people who show up for you when there is nothing in it for them. Allow people the opportunity to have a voice. Listen when they speak, and remember, to create good dialogue that keeps the vibe positive. Don't ever forget the people who help you learn and grow in the beginning. And please don't ever stop building relationships. Sometimes the difference between success and failure is thinking you outgrew the people you once needed. Don't let that person be you. Be loyal to your clients and your clients will be loyal to you. Be loyal to your students and your students will be loyal to you. Be loyal to your friends and family members, and the same will be reciprocated back to you. Even if people mistreat you or do you wrong, leave that up to God. Do the best that you can to present excellence to the world, and you will automatically bring that level of excellence back to you.

CHAPTER 6
PERSEVERANCE

"You may encounter many defeats, but you must not be de- feated. In fact, it may be necessary to encounter the defeats, so you can know who you are, what you can rise from, how you can still come out of it."

—Maya Angelou

THIS CHAPTER TITLE WAS PROBably the easiest one to come up with. I knew as soon as I started writing what I wanted it to be. One word has made the difference for me throughout my entrepreneurial journey. Perseverance. What does it mean to persevere? I'm glad you asked. Perseverance means to stick to it; to not give up. When you persevere, you decide to show up again and again every time you get shut out. Perseverance is the real key to making it, in any industry.

> PERSEVERANCE IS THE REAL KEY TO MAKING IT, IN ANY INDUSTRY.

One of the ways I learned to persevere was by going to the gym on a consistent basis. I developed a level of discipline that made me hungry about stretching myself to the end of myself. Now that I've become accustomed to working out for the last 10 years, it's a habit. I get up and my body automatically tells me, "this is where I need to go." But in the beginning, it was rough. My muscles didn't want to cooperate.

My body was tired. I was always depleted. But when I decided to persevere, I changed everything. I changed my eating habits. I don't eat pork or beef. I really only eat fish now. I also changed my sleeping pattern. I realized if I really want to grind, I need to go to bed early and wake up in the morning. Nothing happens if you don't persevere beyond the resistance, and when I determined in my mind to push past the difficult

> THE WAY I SEE IT, I AM BLESSED TO BE A BLESSING. IF I KNOW IT, AND YOU WANT TO LEARN IT, I'M GOING TO GIVE YOU EVERYTHING I KNOW.

> **YOU'LL NEVER MAKE IT IF YOU KEEP HITTING SNOOZE IN LIFE.**

days, eventually, it all became easier. Now, I work out two times a day. And I look for gym buddies that I can sharpen and help. Most of my gym partners are clients. They come to me for a cut, and then they ask me how to get healthier. You see, I'm not selfish about anything I've learned. The way I see it, I am blessed to be a blessing. If I know it, and you want to learn it, I'm going to give you everything I know. I am going to extend help to you as if you are family, because in my mind you really are. But most people start off excited, they just don't finish strong. When the alarm goes off, they turn off the alarm and go back to bed. You'll never make it if you keep hitting snooze in life. You'll never finish that degree if you keep pushing it back another year. At some point, you've got to decide to do it today as if tomorrow isn't coming.

GET UP QUICK

Earlier in this book, I talked about failing forward. The only way we can really make that happen is through perseverance. Failing forward is all about not stopping when you get stopped. Yes, stops are part of life. You will lose jobs and opportunities. You will mess up deals and lose clients. Life will slap the taste out of your mouth from time to time. But you can't afford to shut down. Even if you get stopped, don't forget where the gas pedal is. Get going again quick.

When I decided to play football, I was looking to get accepted into a D1 school. I had a plan, and I got into school and began to play hard. College was a different experience for me, but I found purpose through my passion. Playing helped me to get through the books and study, and then, as life was happening, an unexpected turn took place. I found out that the lady I was involved with, was pregnant. My daughter would be born a few months after that, and I had to switch up everything to become a father. I thought I was supposed to only focus on football, but fatherhood was an unexpected blessing. This turn shook me at first because it changed my career path a little bit. But I still decided to persevere. Her mom and I were both 16 when she got pregnant, and when she was born, we were 17 years old. Tanajah Green was born on October 9, 2008. It was the best day of my life. She was most beautiful little girl born at UMDNJ hospital. And after she opened her eyes for the first time, a new beginning started for me as well. My daughter's mom and I went to different schools across town from each other. I went to West Side High School in the west ward and she went to Shabazz High School in the south ward. Once she realized she was pregnant she tried to hide it from her parents and me. I didn't know she was actually pregnant until 5 months later, when a friend I played football with (in high school) told me that he saw her on the bus. I said, "Really?" He said, "Yes, and her stomach was big." That's how I found out she was pregnant, and immediately, my aunt reached out to her mother to confirm. Her mom confirmed that she was pregnant, and her family wanted me to drop out of high school to get a job and take care of our child. My aunt went back and forth about me not doing that, and she forced me to persevere in school. My aunt told me I wasn't ready for a child, and she wanted me to focus on going to college to further my education. Meanwhile, my daughter's mom kept denying that she was actually going to go through with it and have the baby. So, there was a lot of back and forth. In the end, I didn't have a say in the matter. My daughter's mom and her mother made the decision, and we had no choice but to figure it out. When my daughter's mom went into labor, I was playing on the field at a football game. Once I got to the locker room, I received a text message saying that she was in labor. I rushed to the hospital after the game, and when I saw my daughter, I knew that her life would radically change my life.

SOMETIMES YOU HAVE TO GIVE UP TO GO UP

> WHEN YOU PERSEVERE, IT DOESN'T MEAN YOU DO EVERYTHING AT THE SAME PACE; IT MEANS YOU PRIORITIZE WHAT MATTERS OVER WHAT DOESN'T MATTER.

I had to make sure that I was a better father than the father I had, so I was willing to give up my temporary dream to be a permanent dad. Even in that, I didn't blame my daughter. I loved her even harder. The situation didn't work out between my daughter's mom and I, but my daughter was a blessing in disguise. I never knew the love a man could have for another human being until I became a dad. I wanted to love her with every part of me, and I tried my best to work, study, and parent all at the same time. When you persevere, it doesn't mean you do everything at the same pace; it means you prioritize what matters over what doesn't matter. I know the parties are popular, but partying shouldn't matter over your family. I know that money is important, but what good would it be to have money, if you have no one to share it with?

LIFE HAPPENED FOR ME, AND IT WILL HAPPEN FOR YOU. BABIES COME UNEXPECTEDLY. JOBS END WITHOUT YOU KNOWING IT.

Perseverance is so important because it sets you apart from the pack. Too many people don't know how to deal with failure or closed doors. Too many people think everything will always work out for them. It's what we hear when we're kids. Most people have been told forever that they are smart and special. And that makes us think that everything will definitely work out for us, especially if we work hard. But the reality is, no matter how good or smart we are, life happens. Life happened for me, and it will happen for you. Babies come unexpectedly. Jobs end without you knowing it. Remember when I talked about being laid off? I wasn't failing. I wasn't doing a bad job. I didn't get fired. The economy just turned on me. And I wasn't ready for it. Most people aren't ready for those moments. We are okay at handling problems that we caused. We understand when we mess up and get caught. But it's hard to deal with a crisis you didn't create. We feel like working hard and doing the right thing should pay off. But sometimes it doesn't. Not at first. That's when perseverance comes in.

BOUNCE BACK

Success doesn't always walk straight into your life. Sometimes success takes some detours. I can't tell you how many times in the early days I thought I was gonna blow up and didn't. So many times I just knew that a new client was gonna mean a new level. So many times I saw a door that I thought was gonna lead to something, and it just led to more struggle. Most of us have had this same kind of path. Graduated and ended up unemployed for six months. Had a great interview but still didn't get the job. Somebody swears they're gonna sign you or help you and it never happens. Most people who are doing something worthwhile have been let down more than they want to admit. And sometimes it happens when you're doing your very best. That's life. But it's not the end of your life. Not unless you stop there. When you hit a roadblock, that's when perseverance comes in. Perseverance is all about playing through, pushing through, staying in the gym.

PHYSICAL FITnESS 101

I alluded to the gym earlier, but now I want to go a little deeper. Why? Because you can learn a lot of life lessons from the gym. So much of my success has to do with the gym. I learn so much while training. At the end of the day, running a business is a lot like training for and running a marathon. The work you have to do to condition your body is the same kind of work you have to do to condition your mind and build your entrepreneurship muscles. Anybody with any real gains in the gym only got them by being consistent. Training is all about consistency. That means you come back even though you're sore. You keep lifting even when you hit the wall. You keep going for the harder reps. Reaching the end of your strength means you find new strength. That's what perseverance is all about.

Finding the discipline to be consistent in the gym and consistent in business has played a major role in my life. The personal sacrifice needed to be a strong businessman isn't easy. And you get better at making those right moves when you get used to making them. Catch that. The more you do, the more you can do. But what gets in the way too often is that people hear no and give up forever. No doesn't mean never. That's why perseverance is so important. When lifting, when building a clientele, when learning a new skill, soreness and setbacks aren't an excuse to give up. It is a hint that you are actually doing something that will make a difference. But it is the repetition that will build muscles and build a business. It is getting up the next day and experiencing the pain again that will solidify gains. Same in building your brand.

ARE WE THERE YET?

A.P.J. Abdul Kalam said "Never stop fighting until you arrive at your destined place - that is, the unique you. Have an aim in life, continuously acquire knowledge, work hard, and have perseverance to realize the great life." If obstacles are still appearing, you're just not finished yet. That's the mindset you have to develop. You have not arrived until you see what you saw. That's why the dream is so important. You have to know what you're aiming for in order to keep persevering. So, to you, I say: get up. Don't hit the snooze button. You're just beginning and you can't give up until you're finished.

CHAPTER 7
TIME IS EVERYTHING

"Be stingy with your time and spend it in spaces that fill you up."

– Janet Mock

SOME PEOPLE SEE ME AS A barber. Some people see me as a trainer. Others see me as a father, and some people consider me a mentor. I appreciate that people tell me that I inspire them, and that my entrepreneurial mindset has encouraged them, but at the core of who I am, I am a leader. And leadership isn't about how many employees you have. It's not about the corporate office you own, or the special perks you get at the nicest hotels and luxury suites. Leadership is influence. By that I mean, you can only inspire people you influence. You can only help people that you influence. And most times, in the Black community especially, I see a lot of us misuse our influence. We tend to focus on all the wrong things. We tend to waste our money on things that don't matter in the long run.

> LEADERSHIP IS INFLUENCE. BY THAT I MEAN, YOU CAN ONLY INSPIRE PEOPLE YOU INFLUENCE.

I know as a kid growing up, one of the reasons gangs were so popular was because kids needed family. They needed community. Everybody didn't have the blessing of a mentor and guidance counselor like I had in Pierre Oscar. Some people just needed to know that somebody cared. When they went home at night, their father wasn't there. Their mother was busy at work. They spent a lot of their days running their own lives, but the gang was a place of safety. I know it's crazy to think of it that way because the violence was very unsafe back then (and even now today), but these kids didn't care about that. If you gave them attention, if you helped them to see something valuable about themselves, they were loyal to you for life. But this kind of influence wasn't good because a lot of them died before their time; they ended up locked up for selling drugs, or they found themselves in a crossfire. I saw it in my own family how bad it could get for people with no direction.

But I had two choices: to become my environment or to change it. I decided to OPEN MY EYES and be a part of the change I want to see in the world. And when I really found my lane as an entrepreneur and as a world-changer, I started using my influence the right way. My question to you is: what do people see in you that makes them want to follow you? Would people say that you influence them to grow up or you influence them to stay where they are? Every person I meet— in the gym, in the shop, on the road, in another country—I want them to see a man of purpose and a man of value. I want them to see someone who plays no games, and wastes no time. Why? Because time waits for no one.

> TIME IS FREE, BUT IT'S PRICELESS. YOU CAN'T OWN IT BUT YOU CAN USE IT.

VALUE YOUR TIME LIKE YOU VALUE YOUR MOnEY

Time is one of the only things you will never get back. Time is what we want most, but what we use worst. Time is free, but it's priceless. You can't own it but you can use it. You can't keep it, but you can spend it. And once you've lost it, you can never get it back. This is why I've learned that if I'm going to succeed, I have to value what I give my energy and time to. That means, I must respect people's time and I must demand that other people

> TELL THE TRUTH AND BE UPFRONT FROM THE BEGINNING

respect my time. Everything doesn't deserve your energy. Even in relationships, if you know that the girl you are dating is not marriage material (and you want to be married within the next 2-3 years) what are you dating her for? What is the end goal? Why invest your time and energy into something that isn't going to work long-term? I ain't knocking you if you just want to chill with somebody. But when you get to the point that you want to build a life and a legacy with somebody, you need to open your eyes and ask different questions. I don't just want to know if you have red bottoms in your closet. I want to know if you have a savings account. I want to know what you think about a blended family, and what your belief system is like. Too many of us go after women for the wrong reason. And then when we have a child, we feel obligated to make something work that wasn't even working when we were in it. Don't let it happen to you. Tell the truth and be upfront from the beginning. Otherwise, you will waste her time and she will waste yours.

BE CONSIDERATE. KEEP YOUR APPOINTMENTS!

When I first started cutting, I had a different mindset about haircuts. I wanted to make as much money as possible and I needed to boost my clientele. So I would tolerate people calling me to get a cut, and not showing up. I would tell people to just walk in and I would take care of them. But that ended up biting me in

> I'M NOT JUST CUTTING HAIR; I'M CREATING A CULTURE. I'M NOT JUST PROVIDING A SERVICE; I AM PROVIDING AN EXPERIENCE.

> IT IS UP TO YOU TO CHANGE THE PATTERN OF YOUR LIFE, AND TO LEAD BY EXAMPLE

the ass. Last year, I changed my approach and shifted my professionalism. I created an app for my business that allowed people to make appointments. I also made sure not to book too many clients in one day so that I didn't overcommit. I try my best to arrive early and leave later than my clients. I think it's rude for your guests to get to your house before you arrive, so I make it a habit to get to my shop before my clients get there. If I'm running late, I send a courtesy text informing my clients of the lateness. I also offer them something to drink when they arrive at the shop, and I am never too prideful to apologize for the inconvenience. I'm not just cutting hair; I'm creating a culture. I'm not just providing a service; I am providing an experience. And most of my clients appreciate my professionalism. Some of them still do not show up even after an appointment, and because time is money, I started a new rule where I charge a no-show fee or a late fee. I didn't create this procedure because I was trying to make more money. I created it so that people could understand the value of my time.

The way I see it, for every no show at the shop, I could've been spending that time with my daughter. I could've been in an online business meeting to learn how to maximize my leadership. I could've slept in and allowed my body to rest; and when people do not respect your time, they also do not respect your craft. It is up to you to change the pattern of your life, and to lead by example.

BUILD YOUR OWn DREAMS

Eventually, I saw a change in my clientele. Some people will fall off because they don't have the same values you have. Don't chase them. Value yourself enough to let them go. But other people will come into your life because they appreciate the customer ser-

> **WHY? BECAUSE IF YOU DON'T BUILD YOUR DREAMS, SOMEONE WILL HIRE YOU TO BUILD THEIRS.**

vice and intentional hospitality. This is the best thing about being a business-owner. I don't have to clock in and clock out for another person. I can create my own schedule, and I can make sure to block out enough time to do things that matter to me: weddings, gym, birthday parties, and quality time with my daughter and family. I'm not knocking anybody who has to work a 9-5. I think it's important to find what works for you, but my question is, how long are you going to do that? What are your future goals? Do you see yourself in that position forever? Even if it's temporary, it doesn't have to be your destiny. I don't think anyone has worked more part-time jobs than me. From work study in school, to KFC and Shoprite; if I know anything, I know how to hustle. I know how to turn two nickels into a dollar. But I never turned a temporary gig into a permanent position. I knew I was there for a quick minute, and I didn't let anything lock me into something I wasn't passionate about. It's all about building your dreams. Your dreams may not look like everybody else's—that's cool. Your goals may not be everybody else's. That's cool. But either way, live each day with your dreams in mind. Why? Because if you don't build your dreams, someone will hire you to build theirs.

SCHEDULE YOUR LIFE AROUnD YOUR GOALS

If you don't have a schedule, you need one. Especially if you want to own your business, and if you want to live your life by your own rules. You need a schedule for everything—what you will eat, when you will sleep, how long you will work, and how long you will enjoy time with family and friends. You also need to schedule a time to *work on it*, and schedule a time to *work in it*. Most people only work in their field, and they never have time to work on their field. So imagine if I never worked *on* my business, I would've never stepped away from cutting hair for 12 hours a day to create a school. The purpose of the school an training center is to duplicate myself. I want to make sure that I build a brand that can go international. And I can't be everywhere at the same time. So I need to carve out time to teach. That's what I mean by working *on it.*

When you only work in it, you become a slave to your passion. When you work on it, you outlive your passion. Working on it also means creating time to dream, imagine, and explore easier ways to make it happen. Don't just work hard; work smart. Now that I have my school in place, I'm teaching new barbers the technique I use because I want my work to outlive me. It is the greatest honor when my clients get to be cut by other

> **WHEN YOU ONLY WORK IN IT, YOU BECOME A SLAVE TO YOUR PASSION. WHEN YOU WORK ON IT, YOU OUTLIVE YOUR PASSION.**

people I taught. Why? Because I am helping somebody else to discover their passion too. All of this connects back to a schedule. One Sunday's, I take the day off. I use that time to reconnect, align, and design. On Monday-Friday, I'm back working, but I carve out time to train and to educate. At night, I'm working on photography, videography, and new products. During the day, I'm building relationships with my clients. On Saturday, I get into the shop as early as 6am, but I leave my last client by 6pm so that I'm not in the shop all night. My point is this: you can design the life you want, and you can have the life you dream— but without being a master of your time, your time will master you!

CHAPTER 8

THE FREEDOM OF FORGIVENESS

It's one of the greatest gifts you can give yourself, to forgive.

Forgive everybody.

— Maya Angelou

FORGIVENESS IS A TOUGH COOKIE TO BITE INTO. IN FACT, when you really get down to the root of it, everybody has dealt with unforgiveness. It's the sting that keeps on stinging, and the hurt that keeps on hurting. It enters in through an insensitive word or a selfish act, but whenever it comes, it's sure to stay for a while. But what I have learned about life is this: we cannot give unforgiveness a key to the door of our lives. It can visit, but eventually, it has to go. I had to learn how to forgive so that I could have the freedom to be who I am. I am stronger now that I've let some things go. I am wiser now that I have let some things go. And most importantly, I can help other people with their problems because I am honest about my path and journey as well; especially when it came to people who let me down in my family. It was hard for me to do at first, but eventually, I needed to admit it, confront it, and then forgive it.

The hardest part is to forgive it, but everything we do, even the hard stuff, is necessary for your personal development. And listen, I get it. But as hard as this chapter may be for you to read, it is necessary and essential. If we are going to really succeed in life, in business, and in our relationships, we must learn the art of forgiveness.

FORGIVENESS IS NOT FORGETTING OR PRETENDING IT DIDN'T HAPPEN.

FORGIVENESS IS NOT MAKING AN EXCUSE FOR UNHEALTHY BEHAVIOR.

WHAT IS FORGIVEnESS?

What is forgiveness? In order to answer that question, let's first talk about what forgiveness is not:

1. *Forgiveness is not forgetting or pretending it didn't happen.* What happened has happened and you will not wake up one day and forget about it. Forgiveness is about learning the lesson without holding onto the pain.

2. *Forgiveness is not making an excuse for unhealthy behavior.* It does not mean to accept what happened as OK. If you have been injured or done wrong, you have a right to be upset about it. But forgiveness is about deciding, "I'm not going to allow your wrong to rob me of my joy."

3. *Forgiveness is not giving people permission to repeat the same behavior.* Just because you forgive someone does not mean you have to live the same way you once lived before the situation occurred. Sometimes, even after forgiving someone, you have to change the relationship so you don't continue to go through what you've been through.

4. *Forgiveness is not restoration.* Forgiving a person doesn't mean the relationship will automatically be restored to the same state. Trust is important in order

FORGIVENESS IS WHEN YOU DECIDE TO LET GO OF RESENTMENT AND BITTERNESS. FORGIVENESS IS WHEN YOU GIVE UP THE NEED TO GET REVENGE.

for any relationship to work. So in order for you to bring people back in your life, trust must be earned. After you forgive, make a decision about who you will allow into your space and who will be a part of your life.

FORGIVInG MY DAD WAS A PROCESS

Knowing what forgiveness is *not* helps us all to know what forgiveness is. Forgiveness is when you decide to let go of resentment and bitterness. Forgiveness is when you give up the need to get revenge. I read a quote that says it like this, "Forgiveness is me giving up my right to hurt you for hurting me."

The reality is, I was hurt by a lot of people in my life, but one of the hardest things to get over was the hurt from my dad. For a long time, I avoided my dad because I felt like he should've been there to help me. I saw my mother struggle and I didn't see him around a lot. He was there, but he really wasn't a father figure to me. He felt like a distant relative, and a lot of things I needed to learn as a child, I figured it out myself. But as I grew, I realized that I needed to let it go. Why? Because I couldn't hold him hostage to who he used to be. My father started coming around more often, and he really tried to make a turn. Even to this day, he will come to the shop and I will cut his hair, and that was a major turn for us. We learned to relate to each other as grown men, and I couldn't keep blaming him for what he didn't do when I was a child.

WHO DO YOU nEED TO FORGIVE?

Even though I'm talking about my dad, I'm sure you also have people in your life that you need to forgive. Why? Because unforgiveness is like carrying a weight on you that's too heavy to carry alone.

> **WHEN YOU FORGIVE, YOU ARE NOT FORGIVING THE OFFENSE, BUT YOU ARE FREEING YOURSELF.**

And remember this: when you forgive, you are not forgiving the offense, but you are freeing yourself. When you hold onto unforgiveness, it can actually bring sickness into your physical body. It limits you and restrains you. You cannot truly have balance and joy if you refuse to let it go. It is a choice, and not a right to not forgive. But I promise you, if you do it, you will be better because of it.

CHECK YOUR FRIENDS

Sometimes, forgiveness means you have to distance yourself from people. I have learned that everyone who starts with you won't finish with you. I wish I could say that all of my high school friends are my close buddies now, but some of them are not. Some people, I had to cut a cord and create a new normal. In life, sometimes we have to distance ourselves from things or people that weigh us down. Every connection is not a good connection. Every relationship isn't meant to last forever. So do yourself a favor and check your circle of friends. Check your partnerships and your family members. And answer these questions to figure out where they belong in your life:

1. Do they help me get to the place where I am going?
2. Are they still doing things that represent who I used to be?
3. Do they tell me what to do without supporting me when I do it?
4. Are they helping me win or encouraging me to lose?
5. Do they get jealous when I am successful?
6. Are they for me or against me?
7. Do they always bring up bad things from my past or do they point me to my future?

Based on the answers to these questions, you know who you need to bring closer and you know who you need to let go of.

PRACTICE WHAT YOU PREACH

Here are a list of practical things you can do to move from resentment to forgiveness.

- Be willing to have tough conversations
  - Don't shut down. Try to have the conversation in a place where you are comfortable and safe.
- Tell the Truth

- Even if the truth hurts them to hear it, tell them the truth anyway. The truth is gonna free you in the end.

- Build new memories
  - If the person is someone you want to rebuild with, then you can't get over the old unless you build the new. Build new memories and try not to bring up the past.

- Be Patient
  - Forgiveness takes time. Give yourself time to heal and then give them time to learn the new you.

- Go to Counseling
  - A lot of people don't go to counseling but it will really help you to move forward. If you don't want to go to counseling, grab a book on forgiveness to help you to move on.

CHAPTER 9
HUSTLE AND MOTIVATION

"To achieve something that you have never achieved before, you must become someone that you have never been before."

–Les Brown

DO YOU KNOW WHAT MAKE THE DIFFERENCE BETWEEN people who take care of business all the time and people who are always looking for an excuse? You ever notice that some people are doers and other people are watchers or talkers? In the end, this usually comes down to two words: intrinsic and extrinsic. These are the two different kinds of motivation that people have. Everybody can be divided into two camps when it comes to what gets them going and keeps them going. Extrinsic motivation means you get motivated from the outside. People who are motivated to do things extrinsically do things when something or somebody causes them to do it. On the job, the people who are mostly extrinsically motivated are the people who only work hard when the supervisor is watching or when somebody gets fired and they are afraid it will be them next. On the other hand, people who are intrinsically motivated do what they need to do because they feel responsible for their work. They work hard because they take pride in their job and want to do well. There is a huge difference between the two kinds of people, and it makes a huge difference in the work environment.

> **I AM RESPONSIBLE FOR MY TIME. I AM RESPONSIBLE FOR TAKING CONTROL OF MY FUTURE.**

THE MOTHER OF ALL HUSTLE

True hustle is intrinsically motivated. It comes from the inside. A hustler starts sentences that really matter with "I." I am responsible for my time. I am responsible for

> **MY MOM WAS MY EXAMPLE. WATCHING HER IN THE HAIR INDUSTRY FOR YEARS TAUGHT ME ABOUT REAL HUSTLE.**

taking control of my future. I have to make something happen for myself and my family. A strong hustle and work ethic starts inside. And certain kinds of businesses require intrinsic motivation and a strong hustle. Hair is one of those. Any business that needs customers is gonna mean you need to know how to sell yourself and your service of product. Some people think that means that only certain people can be successful. That's not really true. Some people think it means that you have to have a certain personality to make it. That's not true. All kinds of people can learn how to build their clientele and get attention. Even if you're an introvert, you can work on some things that will work anyway. It's gonna be harder if you're not naturally a people person or a talker, but all of that can be developed. It starts with having the motivation to do it.

I know exactly where my hustle started: Ameina Edwards. My mom was my example. Watching her in the hair industry for years taught me about real hustle. When I was born, she was 22. She already had my brother Orlando Jamar. My little sister Mahogany was born five years after me. My mom was our rock. She did hair, but she wasn't just your normal, everyday stylist. She was amazing. She is where I got my vision from of what I wanted to be and do. She was the best at everything she did, and she did it all. Every morning she would drop us off at school at Madison Avenue Elementary and Thurgood Marshall in Irvington. Then she headed to work at the salon, Max's in Newark. My mother was the only black woman at that shop among all latino women; but they loved her! Around 3:00 she would come pick us up from school and take us back to the salon. We did our homework there while she worked. In those days I learned how important it is to work hard and become the best you can at what you do. I watched her master her craft on those afternoons after school in the shop. And I learned how important it was to hustle all around. Mom didn't just do a great job with us and at work. She also was a rapper on top of it all. One of the best in Jersey. She did collabos with Lauryn Hill and Wyclef. She could do anything! But hair was her passion. It's like it was in her blood. I guess I should say it's in **our** blood.

I learned from her that nobody was gonna give me anything. I had to go and get it for myself. The lessons kept coming after she died when I was 9. Nobody was really trying to keep all three of us so we went through some hell. Sometimes it felt like family didn't want to be bothered and we felt unwelcome everywhere. It meant I bounced around and left home as early as I could. Ever since then my goal has been to build as much as I can on my own terms and make sure I have my own thing to depend on. It all turned into fuel, motivation. Motivation makes all the difference in the world. Waiting around for somebody else to fix something is the best way to waste your time and your potential. Letting hard times stop you is the best way to end up with nothing. No matter what's happening on the outside, maintain your fire on the inside. That's the kind of intrinsic motivation that will last.

WHAT DID YOU SAY?

When talking about motivation and hustle we can't forget the mental part of it. One of my favorite quotes is "He who says he can and he who says he can't are both usually right." It means that what you do or don't do starts with you. What you become or don't become starts with you. Do you always talk about what you can't do and how impossible it is going to be to work your dream and vision? If so, that negative energy impacts your whole body and it impacts the people around you. It makes you spend too much energy worrying and not enough planning. Then people hear it and they become less likely to invest in you or partner with you. Nobody wants to buy into something if you don't even sound like you believe. On the other hand, thinking and talking positively can change your whole world for the better. Scientists have figured out that the movie you play over and over in your head about yourself is going to turn into real life eventually. So if you are constantly planning the next big move and telling yourself how close you are to your break, it is drawn to you. And the more you think and talk like a champion, the more it gives you the energy of a champion. Positivity is contagious and powerful. This means that hustle isn't just about what you do, it starts with what you think and say.

> ONE OF MY FAVORITE QUOTES IS "HE WHO SAYS HE CAN AND HE WHO SAYS HE CAN'T ARE BOTH USUALLY RIGHT."

> TRUE HUSTLE DOESN'T STOP IN YOUR HEAD. IT THEN CONNECTS TO A PLAN

GET SMART

True hustle doesn't stop in your head. It then connects to a plan. A plan is what makes hustle effective. Too many people just spin their wheels all day and get nowhere. That's because they aren't in drive, they're still parked in neutral. Creating a plan with short term and long term goals and executing it is what makes hustle make sense. Working harder is never better than working smarter and working in the right direction.

> **TAKE TIME, STUDY YOUR CRAFT, SHARE THE VISION AND DON'T EVER STOP HUSTLING.**

Always try to use SMART goals in life. That's a piece of advice that will always pay off. SMART goals are Specific, Measurable, Achievable, Relevant and Time-bound. Make sure that everything you think about doing, you first run it through this system. So if you want to build your clientele, hustle alone isn't gonna do it if it's not SMART hustle. Spending $1,000 on Facebook and Instagram ads isn't gonna do it automatically. You have to be specific (So make sure you target your ads to men in the age group you want, who live in the cities you want to penetrate and who list interests that match your brand and style). You also need to be measurable (Make sure you pay attention to the analytics the platforms give you on the ads each day to be sure you are hitting the number of people you want for the money invested). Also, make sure your goal is achievable (Don't set a goal to reach 1,000 new clients next week, it's not gonna happen.) Stay relevant with your effort (Don't put up an ad that asks people to listen to your favorite artist or that talks about everything but your business). And last, keep what you do timely or time-bound (Set a specific window of when you will run the ads and how long. Maybe consider running them during a major event in the city when people will be in town and needing a cut).

Take time, study your craft, share the vision and don't ever stop hustling. This is the formula. But the drive to follow it and add your own sauce to make something amazing comes from the inside.

CHAPTER 10
MANIFEST THE VISION

"Some people want it to happen, some wish it would happen, and others make it happen."

- Michael Jordan

IN CHAPTER 4 I WROTE A LOT ABOUT HAVING A DREAM and letting it drive your success. I want to talk in this chapter about having and sticking with a vision too. Dreams and visions are similar, but what I really want to talk about here is how the vision needs to be something that's alive and that won't go away. Dreams happen while we're asleep. A dream might not be realistic and might not be real. A dream can be crazy and off the wall. It's just something you get and that inspires your imagination. But a vision is something with weight and reality to it. A vision is about seeing something that isn't touchable yet, but that can definitely be made real. To make it make more sense, a dream is like a wish and a vision is like a plan. Both of them are about the future and possibilities. But a vision is like a dream with work boots on. It is what you can actually move on.

I remember when I first mapped out my vision. After some years of cutting part-time it started looking like my cutting was gonna take off. I was working at Flii Nation Barber Suite and my clientele was starting to build. I started to realize what I wanted my daily to look like. I started thinking about travelling and having big name clients. I started realizing I had learned about the best techniques and that I could share what I had picked up. I started seeing a vision. Like I said in the last chapter, the more I started hustling and really building my motivation, the more I could

> **A REAL VISION ISN'T SOMETHING THAT JUST COMES WHILE YOU SLEEP LIKE A DREAM. IT'S SOMETHING THAT KEEPS YOU WIDE AWAKE AND WORKING.**

visualize the future. It was like when I closed my eyes I could see myself on planes flying all over and sitting in networking events across the country. Having this vision helped me know when I was moving in the right direction and kept me hungry for what was coming.

> **ONCE THE VISION STARTS COMING TO YOU, YOU HAVE TO DO THE WORK TO MAKE IT START HAPPENING.**

The vision wasn't just a pipe dream though. That's important to get. A real vision isn't something that just comes while you sleep like a dream. It's something that keeps you wide awake and working. Every time I saw myself putting up a viral post in my mind, it made me work that much harder on how I wrote my posts. Every time I visualized myself cutting a celebrity, it made me raise my game professionally with customers.

When you get a real vision you start to see how far you are from where you need to be. You have to work to get there. You have to get rid of the distance between what you are now and what you know you can be.

MAnIFEST YOUR DESTInY

A word you have to know is manifesting. Writers who write about positive thinking always talk about how important it is to manifest things. Manifesting something means to maintain positive energy, believe that something is possible, and visualize it until it happens. You have to manifest your

> **THE THING ABOUT VISION IS YOU WILL NEVER SEE THE WHOLE THING BEFORE IT HAPPENS.**

vision. Once the vision starts coming to you, you have to do the work to make it start happening. That's not just the kind of work you might think about. It means heart work/head work and not just hand work. If you have a vision of owning a multi-million dollar business, you have to manifest it. Start learning from multi-million dollar business owners. Think of the name and logo. Draw up a business plan. Have business cards made even if you think you're not ready for them. Put up a mock license or certificate or degree until you get the real one. Thank God every night for opening up the door. This is manifesting.

I remember how much I wanted to travel back before KIH really hit hard. Traveling was one of the main things I saw in my vision. So back before I started really travelling much, I started getting ready. I started researching entrepreneurs who were on the level I wanted to be on, especially in the hair industry. I started looking into pro tips for people who travel all the time. I was researching different networking events and major industry spots before I was able to go to them. I started thinking through opportunities and issues travelling could cause. I knew what I wanted to do and so I got ready. If you believe something, act like you believe.

YOU DOn'T KnOW UnTIL YOU KnOW

The thing about vision is you will never see the whole thing before it happens. Even if you have a strong vision and you feel ready, you never know everything until you're in it. So with traveling, some stuff I wasn't ready for until I got on the road. It ended up being a whole different lifestyle and taking a different perspective. Being

KEEP THE MAIN THING THE MAIN THING: WHEN YOU ARE TRAVELLING FOR BUSINESS, IT'S BUSINESS.

in airports and different cities a lot can get hard sometimes. You have to keep that motivation going and remember your hustle. And temptations come with the manifestation. Part of my brand is health and wellness. But when you're travelling a lot and constantly on the road, it gets easy to cut back on the things that made you successful in the first place. Being places late at night and nothing but fast food places open. Not taking the time to get to the gym in the city you're in because of scheduling. Forgetting the things that built your brand is dangerous when the vision starts manifesting itself. You have to see travelling, and every new level of your vision, as a challenge. Every time something new happens it is a challenge to double down on the vision and the hustle. I believe that life gives us tests all the time. Things happen to see what we are, where we are and what we're ready for. So you have to be consistent even when things get crazy.

TIPS FOR TRAVEL

If you know you want to do something kind of like what I do and travel a lot, you have to have some rules and guidelines.

ALWAYS BE PREPARING FOR THE NEXT ONE.

It's too easy to get lazy or get caught up in the opportunities and the temptations. So do some things that set yourself up for success and not failure.

OPEN EYES

1. Keep the main thing the main thing: When you are travelling for business, it's business. Know how to focus on your vision and not get caught up with the women and partying. Take care of business and everything else will fall into place.

2. Stick with the routine: If you go to the gym four days a week at home, go four days a week when on the road. If you stick to a specific diet at home, take care of your temple on the road too.

3. Don't waste connections: Like I said earlier in this book, your network is your net worth. Whenever you are at networking events or meeting people, treat it like you're on the job. Make the best first impression every time. This means treat each trip like you're on an interview the whole time. You never know who is going to refer you or open a door that can change your life.

4. Always be preparing for the next one: Travelling is something you have to learn how to do well. As you start with it make sure you're getting better each trip. Invest in some good luggage, garment bags and stuff like that. Register for TSA Pre-Check and join a frequent flyer program. If you're gonna do it, do it well.

CHAPTER 11
KEEPING IT HANDSOME

"Some things are good for our image but bad for our pockets."

—Mokokoma Mokhonoana

WATCH YOUR HABITS. HABITS WILL MAKE AND BREAK you in anything. Develop enough good habits and watch the success come. Pick up enough bad habits and it's only a matter of time before it all comes crashing down. We all recognize this in most areas of life. If you can choose between a doctor who usually sees you five minutes after you get into the office versus a doctor who always makes you wait over an hour, who are you choosing? Are you more likely to talk to the girl who is always sweet and easy to deal with or the one who is constantly negative? Tomorrow at lunch time are you going to pick up food from the spot where the food is always hot and the service is great, or from that spot where they always make you pull up to wait on fries and they still end up cold? We watch people's habits. And we make decisions about them based on their habits. It's human nature. It's how we make smart decisions and predict what is probably gonna happen if we choose to do a certain thing. For some reason we know that as consumers, but we forget the power of habits when we are the business owner or the employee. Or even more dangerous: sometimes in business we don't know which habits are good and bad for our brand and bottom line until it's too late.

SOMETIMES IN BUSINESS WE DON'T KNOW WHICH HABITS ARE GOOD AND BAD FOR OUR BRAND AND BOTTOM LINE UNTIL IT'S TOO LATE.

KEEPInG IT In PERSPECTIVE

How did I come up with the name Keeping It Handsome? My mother. She inspired me with everything, and the name of my business was no different. Every morning, when my mother saw me, she would say "hey handsome." Or when I got ready for school, she would look over at me and say, "you look so handsome." And I remember how that made me feel.

> ABOUT 595,000 BUSINESSES CLOSE EVERY YEAR TOO. THIS MEANS THAT EVERY DAY IN THIS COUNTRY ON AVERAGE ALMOST 2,000 BUSINESSES ARE STARTING.

When someone calls you handsome, you feel like you are on top of the world; and a man's confidence is his greatest asset. Even if you don't have the world, you feel like you're on top of it. And that's what I wanted every client to feel. I wanted to restore the dignity and integrity of manhood. I wanted men, everywhere, to feel like they can be whatever they want to be. And that's why I call my brand "Keeping it Handsome."

The brand of "Keeping it Handsome" has kept me motivated to maintain the right habits for a long time. Long before those words came around, when I couldn't even describe in words what I felt and wanted to do, I knew I had to be careful. You don't want to make the mistake of killing your vision and dream early by carelessness. Before I ever owned much of anything, I knew I had to take care of spaces I was using, even when it wasn't mine. I learned early on not to rush somebody's cut just because I wanted to get home or hit the town.

OPEN EYES

Daily habits like respecting customers and paying attention to detail are what KIH is built on.

Part of what has kept me committed to good habits is knowing how stiff the competition is. The Small Business Administration says that over 627,000 new businesses are started every year in the United States. About 595,000 businesses close every year too. This means that every day in this country on average almost 2,000 businesses are starting. That's a lot of competition. Especially when you think about how many of them are in the same few industries. Hair has always been big business for Black people. That's why the first self-made Black millionaire, Madame C.J. Walker, made her money in hair. There were 650,000 barbers and cosmetologists in the United States in 2014 and African Americans spent $473 million on haircare in 2017.

It's a huge industry and one that many people think is easy and pays well without requiring a lot of education. That means that people run and buy clippers and rent booths every day. Competition is huge. That means people in our industry can't afford bad habits. People have too many choices to excuse a bad experience. When they walk into a dirty shop, people will walk right back out. If you don't have your tools well-maintained and sanitary, people don't want to deal with you. Dusty brushes and combs not in Barbasol isn't gonna cut it. Think about it: We use razors and come into contact with people's skin. Ringworms, infections, all kinds of things can go wrong if a barber isn't sanitary, careful,

OUR PROFESSIONAL HABITS AREN'T THE ONLY ONES THAT HAVE TO BE WATCHED. YOU'VE GOTTA KEEP AN EYE ON YOUR MONEY HABITS TOO.

well-trained and paying attention. Habits matter. People don't want to watch you talk with friends who come by and eat fish sandwiches for 15 minutes while they sit in the chair waiting. Habits matter. You don't have the only chair in town.

Part of what kept me motivated for a long time was imagining that I was behind. I knew I didn't want to be one of the thousands of people who close up shop every day. So I always kept things in perspective and remembered the numbers.

FROM BARBER CHAIR TO BAnK BOOK

Our professional habits aren't the only ones that have to be watched. You've gotta keep an eye on your money habits too. I could write a whole book about this one. If you want to be big time, you have to make sure you are taking care of the financial end of things. Too many good people with great ideas and skills lose it all here. Money matters matter. First off, don't play with Uncle Sam. Barbers and cosmetologists mess up all the time over taxes. Find somebody who knows how to keep you above board with this. With new technology this is getting better for a lot of us, but ours is still a cash business for the most part. That tempts some people to make stupid decisions. Know the tax laws or have somebody who will know them for you. Put your tax money aside every month and put it where you know you won't touch it. If you own your own and are considered self-employed, know what that means for you.

Also, barbers need insurance and savings just like everybody else. Don't be the one with the best cars and a banging system, but nothing saved for retirement or no money to be buried when you die. Nothing lasts forever. Just because you're hot today and the money is flowing doesn't mean it will be like that forever. Do more planning than just making a pile for each bill at the end of the week on your bed. What about saving? What about investing? Money has a habit of disappearing unless you tell it what to do. Either have a plan for your finances or plan to wonder at the end of every month what happened to all of your money.

THERE'S An APP FOR THAT

Too many people get nervous whenever they here the word investing. Most people think they don't have enough money to invest or are intimidated about where to start. It's the 21st Century now so neither of those excuses work. Saving and investing is as simple as downloading an app now.

> **IF YOU DON'T BUDGET YOU WILL SPEND WAY MORE THAN YOU THINK YOU WILL AND WON'T KNOW WHERE IT WENT.**

First let's talk about some basics. A budget is a necessity. That means you should be deciding where you spend your money before you actually spend it. If you don't budget you will spend way more than you think you will and won't know where it went. Start the process by going back over your bank account statements for the past three months. Add up how much you spent on fast food and liquor. Add up how much you spent on that last trip. Add up how much money is auto-drafted out of your account each month for subscription services that you don't use and some you even forgot you even have.

Pay attention. Then go online and find a good sample budget you want to use.

> Tip: A good budget usually keeps needs (rent or mortgage, utilities, food, medicine, etc.) down to no more than 40% and wants (entertainment, trips, restaurants, clubbing, etc.) down to no more than 30%. Also add in saving 10%, giving 10% and investing 10%.

When it comes to how to save and invest there are apps and services at your bank or credit union that can make it easy. If you're just starting out with saving, consider setting up automatic drafts to your savings account from your checking account every month. It's easier to save money when you don't have to be the one to move it. Also, if you are on direct deposit you can have part of the money go directly to savings without you ever even seeing it in your checking. If you need an app to help you with saving download Acorns. It helps you save easily by rounding up every purchase you make and putting the change into an account. So, for instance, if you buy something for $3.91 Acorns will take the $0.09 and put it into your Acorns account. Some checking accounts at certain banks will do the same thing. As soon as the change adds up to $5.00 the app will start automatically investing the money into investments you choose or you can just let it choose based on your investment needs (age, income level, etc.)

Also, if you want to get started on investing check out these apps: Vanguard, Robinhood, and Stash. You can start small on these platforms with small amounts, limited fees and a lot of information to help you start learning. Starting small is okay, it pays off over time. Also, using a money manager might make sense for a lot of people. If you think it will be too expensive or that you don't have enough money for it to make sense, think again. Many banks and credit unions offer wealth management services for free to account holders. Your personal bank or credit union is also often a great place to find a business loan because of the relationship you have built (credit unions are especially great for loans – credit cards, car loans, unsecured loans, mortgages, business loans, etc.)

> **PUT THE TIME IN RESEARCHING CREDIT, INSURANCE AND RETIREMENT IN PARTICULAR.**

KnOWLEDGE IS POWER

There are some things you should definitely know as you start cleaning up your financial habits. Put the time in researching credit, insurance and retirement in particular. Use the info below to get started.

Credit: Your credit score may be the most important number in your life. Take control of it. Sign up for free credit monitoring on sites like www.creditkarma.com and www.creditsesame.com. Also, be sure to get your free credit report from each of the three credit bureaus (Experian, Equifax and TransUnion) each year through www.annualcreditreport.com. If you really want to work on your credit, spend a good amount of time on www.creditboards.com learning how to build and fix your credit.

Insurance: Spend time researching the difference between term and whole life insurance. If you are a business owner, make sure all of your insurances are up to date and make sense for you each year.

Retirement: Spend time researching the difference between an IRA and a Roth IRA. Also know the difference between a 401K and a Roth 401K (There are huge differences when it comes to taxes).

CHAPTER 12
THE MARATHON CONTINUES

"The fight is won or lost far away from witnesses — behind the lines, in the gym, and out there on the road, long before I dance under those lights."

–Muhammad Ali

A GOOD BUSINESSMAN MAKES IT look easy. Part of my job is to do what I do so well that it looks easy. But don't let looks fool you. No one ever became great only doing what was easy. Neither will you. Building a brand, developing a culture, changing your life, manifesting the vision, staying motivated, all of it will be hard. It takes work to work the vision. And it doesn't end. You don't one day wake up and say I'm a success now, I'm done. "Making it" is a marathon, not a sprint.

> **"MAKING IT" IS A MARATHON, NOT A SPRINT.**

When a runner is preparing for a marathon, they know they have to do things different than somebody running a 100-meter dash. If you are only gonna be running for 15 seconds, pacing and breathing and stamina won't be that important. But that's not how a career works. A marathon is about 26 miles, not 26 seconds. Discipline matters. Timing matters. KIH didn't happen with one good cut or one good year. You have to keep doing the right thing, the right way and getting the right results over and over again. Plus, you have to have the right motivation because most of it is gonna happen in the dark with nobody watching. And it's gonna seem like it's not important at the time.

> **YOU HAVE TO KEEP DOING THE RIGHT THING, THE RIGHT WAY AND GETTING THE RIGHT RESULTS OVER AND OVER AGAIN.**

JUST GETTInG STARTED

Everything I have laid out here isn't the end of the story. The process doesn't end here, you have to continue to grow within yourself and continue the process. Take these words to heart, but know that you can't just read this book like an instruction manual. You can't just do each thing I mentioned once and then sit this book down and wait for success. This is a never-ending process. Read, do and repeat. You can't leave out the "repeat" part. Implement over and over again. That means that celebrations should never last too long. One of the mistakes some people make is that when they level up, they spend too long celebrating and take forever to get back to achieving. Each new client, each new platform, each open door is an invitation to sweat more and work harder. If you do, it multiplies. If you don't it evaporates.

Another important thing to know is that every person's course is different. Depending on what industry you're in and what your vision is, you will have to work differently than me. So, part of the work is paying attention to where you are and who you are. Some people need to spend a lot of time on branding and marketing early on because they are in a market that's full and it's hard to differentiate (that just means to get noticed and get business). Some people need to spend all of their time building skills and connections early on. You might be ready to buy your own space in two years and somebody else might not be ready for ten years. Each person's process is different. But like any area of life, there are some rules everybody needs to know.

RULES OF THE RACE

Since building a successful brand and business is like a marathon and not a sprint, it is good to know the rules of marathon-running. Runner's World magazine put together "10 Golden Rules of Marathon Success" and they might help you get going. Here are seven of them, adapted for business success.

1. Warm up and cool down: It's tempting to jump right into your run, but don't. A five- to 10-minute warmup raises your heart and breathing rates and gets blood flowing to muscles. Insert a few strides to wake up your nervous system and get fast- twitch muscle fibers firing. **In general, the faster or farther you intend to go, the more you should warm up.**

   The same thing works in business. It's important to always take the time to plan out what you are gonna do, do the research and take the necessary time to make sure you are going to be able to succeed. It's not about getting started quickly, it's about taking the time to start right so you can finish well.

2. Start slow, build gradually: Coaches say the best way to avoid injury is to follow the 10-percent rule: Increase your weekly mileage and the length of your long run by no more than 10 percent each week. Your muscles and joints need time to adapt to the workload.

Don't think you have to have everything figured out right away and be a mogul overnight. Build, learn, grow. Time is your friend. Do yourself a favor and give yourself permission to adjust to the learning curve.

> **DON'T THINK YOU HAVE TO HAVE EVERYTHING FIGURED OUT RIGHT AWAY AND BE A MOGUL OVERNIGHT.**

3. Hit the hills: Once a week during the first half of your training, run the hilliest route you can find. Hill work builds leg strength, aerobic capacity, and running economy (how efficiently your body uses oxygen), which gives you the strength and stamina to run faster later in the program.

Get used to obstacles early on. Sometimes success happens to people too quick and they start thinking the whole journey will be like that. It's best to get ready for hill and hard moments early. Eventually you are gonna struggle, lose clients, experience personal issues, etc. Don't convince yourself that everything will be easy or fun, prepare for some pain.

4. Alternate hard and easy: If you don't push yourself, you'll never develop the ability to run farther or faster. But if you don't rest enough, you'll burn out or get injured. Follow speed sessions or long runs with an easy run or rest day, and

> **REST AND ENJOY LIFE SOMETIMES. PEOPLE ARE NOT MACHINES; WE NEED TO HAVE FUN AND GET SLEEP AND ENJOY FAMILY AND FRIENDS.**

every few weeks cut back your mileage by 20 percent. These recovery periods allow your body to repair and rebuild damaged muscle tissue, thereby helping you get stronger and more resistant to fatigue at faster paces and longer distances.

Rest and enjoy life sometimes. People are not machines; we need to have fun and get sleep and enjoy family and friends. There is no reason to work yourself into an early grave or look back over your life and realize all you ever did was work, sleep and then get right back to it. What are you working toward? What are you working for? Your life should have a bigger reason for being than just making a few dollars. Hustle, but don't hurt yourself!

5. Remember to cross-train: When you run, your muscles, joints, and connective tissues absorb a lot of shock. Cross-training gives your body a break from the pounding while maintaining your cardiovascular fitness. Yoga, Pilates, and strength training promote recovery, build muscle, and develop a strong upper body. Swimming, cycling, elliptical training, and rowing improve your aerobic fitness.

Keep all of your life sharp. Don't just focus on being a better barber or businessman. All of you is connected. Keeping your mind tight is gonna be important for your business. Same with

> **KEEP ALL OF YOUR LIFE SHARP. DON'T JUST FOCUS ON BEING A BETTER BARBER OR BUSINESSMAN**

training and exercise. Work hard for balance. Being stronger mentally, spiritually and emotionally will all help you to be better professionally.

> **PUT IN THE TIME AND STAY MOTIVATED.**

6. Measure your effort: Go too hard on easy days and you won't have the energy for speed sessions and long runs. Go too slow during hard workouts and you won't push your fitness to the next level. Use pace, heart rate, or the talk test to ensure you're working out at the right intensity and reaping the intended benefit of every run.

   Find the right combo for you. Your perfect mix of work, rest, enjoyment and development is gonna be different than other people. Pay attention to what you need to be healthy and successful. It's good to watch other people's strategies, but know your own needs. Set your day off for when it makes sense for you. Make hours that you can handle.

7. Run at race pace: Spend time practicing your goal speed during training and it will feel like your body's natural rhythm come race day. Mentally, logging dozens of miles at race pace will help you feel more confident when the starting gun goes off.

   Anybody who has played a sport has heard some version of this. Basically, practice full out. Do in practice what you're gonna do on game day. That means never treat any cut, any event, and opportunity like it's minor. Put in the time every time.

OPEN EYES

As you build, work these general rules and watch things happen. No matter what part of the country or world you're in, no matter what your concept or industry is, work works. Put in the time and stay motivated. Before you know it you will have trained yourself into a champion in every area of life. Keep it handsome!

Printed in the USA
CPSIA information can be obtained
at www.ICGtesting.com
CBHW050553271124
18025CB00047B/875